Contents

Language Arts

Social Studies

Math

Science

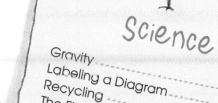

© 2000 School Zone Publishing Company

School's Out!

A **compound** word is two words put together to make a new word.

Most of the time, the meaning of the compound word is similar to the combined meanings of the smaller words. But sometimes the meaning of a compound word is different than you'd think. After all, there's no pepper in a peppermint!

Look at each kid's summer to-do list. Circle the compound words each uses.

Kelsey

Lie in the sunshine
Buy a camp sweatshirt
Find starfish at the seashore
Send lots of postcards
Catch fireflies in the woods
Take time to daydream

Al

Forget about homework!
Catch grasshoppers in the yard
Play basketball
Watch the fireworks
Eat watermelon
Swim every afternoon

Matt

Practice with my skateboard
Play baseball every day
Have a campfire at the beach
Go downtown to see skyscrapers
Have a backyard camping trip
Invite my friends to my birthday party

Tori

Go out in a rowboat
Take junior lifeguard lessons
Play flashlight tag
Spend a weekend at the fair
Grow some huge sunflowers
Sit on the porch during a thunderstorm

Rhyming Words

Have some summertime fun with **hink-pinks**. A hink-pink is a pair of rhyming one-syllable words that describes something. Read each of the riddles below. Then think of a word that rhymes with the boldfaced word and answers the riddle. Write the word on the line and you'll have a hink-pink!

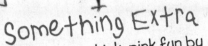

1. Where does a dandelion come from?

   It grows from a **weed** _____.

2. Where does water from the clouds go?

   It goes down a **rain** _____.

3. What do you need if your shorts get wet?

   You need a **spare** _____.

4. What do you call a gloomy Monday?

   It is a **gray** _____.

5. What is another name for a sunny bed?

   It is called a **hot** _____.

6. What do you get if you put ice in the lake?

   You get a **cool** _____.

7. What do you call a covering for a hurt knee?

   It is a **scratch** _____.

Did You Know?

A pair of rhyming lines is called a couplet. Three rhyming lines are called a triplet. Which is this?

My dog sat upon the bed;
Slowly lifted up his head—
"Feed me, please!" is what he said.

8. What do you get if you dam up a river?

   You get a **fake** _____.

_____

Problems at the Zoo

June is National Zoo Month. So any day in June is a perfect time to head off to the nearest zoo. In each zoo sign, write the number of each type of animal.

There are many symbols used in mathematics. Here are some you probably already know.

+ plus	− minus
= equal to	≠ not equal to
x multiplied by	÷ divided by
< less than (2<3)	> greater than (3>2)

In each equation below, substitute numbers for the animal names according to the zoo map. If the number sentence is true, write **yes** on the line. If it isn't true, write **no**. Be sure you solve each equation by starting at the left and completing one step at a time.

1. monkeys – elephants = wolves

   _____ – _____ = _____   _____

2. monkeys + panda – snakes = wolves

   _____ + _____ – _____ = _____   _____

3. wolves + panda = monkeys

   _____ + _____ = _____   _____

4. camels + panda = wolves – giraffe

   _____ + _____ = _____ – _____   _____

5. lions x giraffe < camels

   _____ x _____ < _____   _____

6. panda > giraffe

   _____ > _____   _____

7. wolves + giraffe ≠ elephants + camels

   _____ + _____ ≠ _____ + _____   _____

8. elephants x lions + camels = monkeys

   _____ x _____ + _____ = _____   _____

9. monkeys ÷ lions ≠ camels

   _____ ÷ _____ ≠ _____   _____

Solving Equations

Zoo-ables

When counting syllables in a word, don't be fooled by the number of vowels. The number of syllables is the same as the number of vowel *sounds* you hear, not the number of vowels.

Say each animal's name. Then write the number of vowels you hear in the box by the animal's picture.

giraffe

monkey

rhinoceros

elephant

snake

lion

panda

hippopotamus

seal

peacock

camel

hyena

Did You Know?

The word zoo is short for zoological garden. The world's first zoological garden opened in Vienna, Austria, in 1765. New York City's Central Park Zoo is the oldest zoo in the United States. It opened in 1864.

ABC Sign-Up

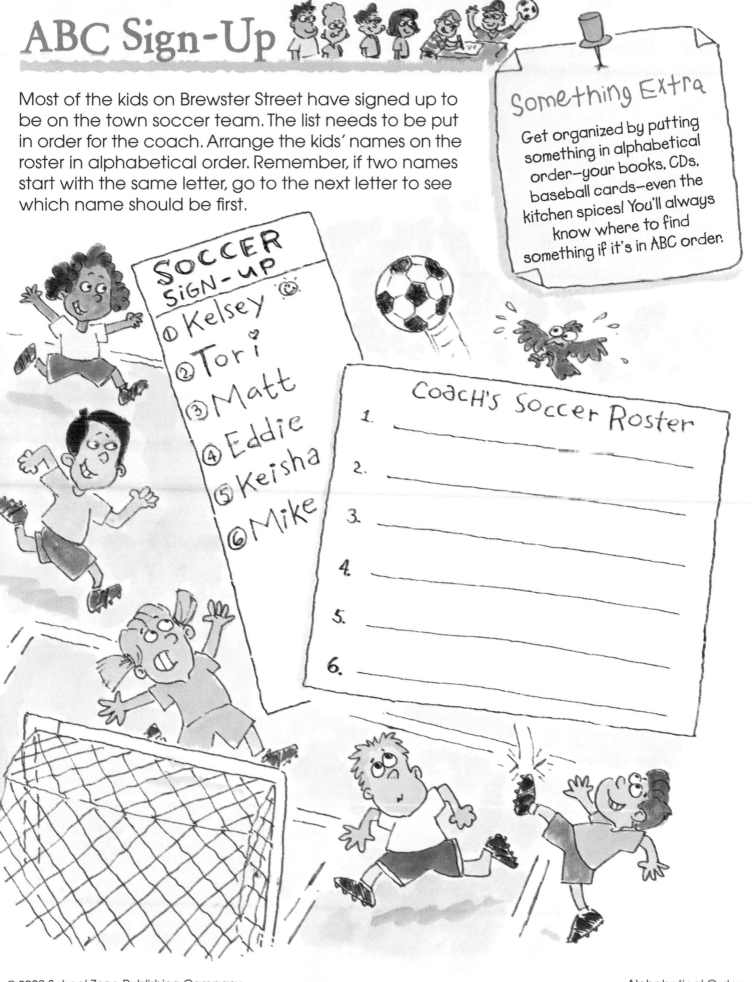

Most of the kids on Brewster Street have signed up to be on the town soccer team. The list needs to be put in order for the coach. Arrange the kids' names on the roster in alphabetical order. Remember, if two names start with the same letter, go to the next letter to see which name should be first.

Something Extra

Get organized by putting something in alphabetical order—your books, CDs, baseball cards—even the kitchen spices! You'll always know where to find something if it's in ABC order.

SOCCER SIGN-UP

1. Kelsey
2. Tori
3. Matt
4. Eddie
5. Keisha
6. Mike

Coach's Soccer Roster

1. _____
2. _____
3. _____
4. _____
5. _____
6. _____

Summer Survey

Millions of people watch World Cup soccer matches on television. A survey gives us this information.

A **survey** is a question or several questions asked of a group of people. There are surveys that ask people about television shows they watch, foods they eat, stores they prefer, and who they want to vote for. The answers give the survey takers the information they want.

Take a survey. Find out which summer sports your friends and family members most like to play and watch. Ask seven people for their opinions. Record their answers on the survey form below.

> ## Something Extra
> Think of another survey idea. Write one or two questions you want to ask. Then decide who to survey. Record your answers and see what they tell you.

Person being surveyed	Favorite sport to watch	Favorite sport to play

1. According to your survey, which sport is the favorite to watch? _____

2. Which sport is the favorite to play? _____

3. How many adults did you survey? _____

4. How many children or teenagers did you survey? _____

5. Did most adults choose the same sports as younger people did? _____

Make a Goal!

Set yourself a summertime goal of knowing the basic multiplication facts. Here are some facts to practice. Write each answer on the soccer ball with its fact.

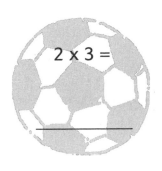

2 x 3 = _____

3 x 4 = _____

5 x 5 = _____

7 x 2 = _____

8 x 3 = _____

3 x 7 = _____

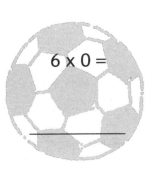

6 x 0 = _____

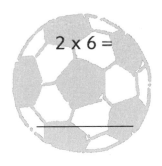

2 x 6 = _____

2 x 9 = _____

8 x 1 = _____

4 x 6 = _____

3 x 5 = _____

4 x 4 = _____

5 x 2 = _____

Did You Know?

If you listen to the news or read the newspaper, the term "Gallup Poll" may be familiar to you. The Gallup Poll is a kind of survey. The poll was started by a man named George Gallup, who founded the American Institute for Public Opinion in 1935.

Plotting a Garden

The Brewster Street kids are planting a garden in Al's backyard. They will share the work of planting, weeding, and picking their crops. First, they have to decide how much space to use for each plant.

Perimeter is a measurement of shapes. Perimeter measures the distance around the outside of a shape. To find the perimeter of a rectangle, add the lengths of all four sides.

Study the garden plan. Inside each section, write its perimeter in feet.

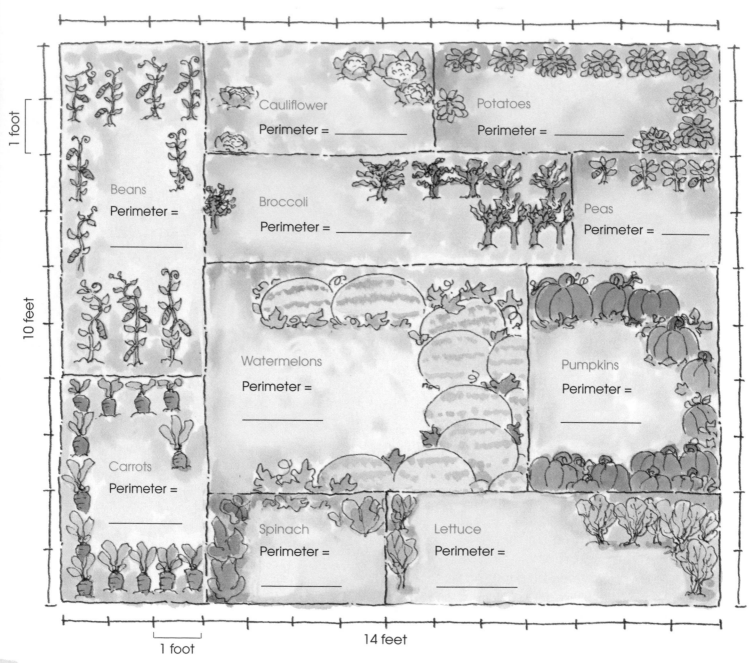

1 foot

10 feet

Beans

Perimeter = _____

Cauliflower

Perimeter = _____

Potatoes

Perimeter = _____

Broccoli

Perimeter = _____

Peas

Perimeter = _____

Watermelons

Perimeter = _____

Pumpkins

Perimeter = _____

Carrots

Perimeter = _____

Spinach

Perimeter = _____

Lettuce

Perimeter = _____

1 foot

14 feet

1. Which type of vegetable has the greatest perimeter? the least?

_____   _____

2. What is the perimeter of the watermelon patch?

_____

3. Which has the greatest perimeter, cauliflower or spinach? By how much?

_____   _____

4. Which has the greatest perimeter, pumpkins or lettuce? By how much?

_____   _____

5. If the kids want to put a fence around the entire garden, how many feet of fencing will they need?

_____

6. How many feet of fencing will surround the spinach and the lettuce?

_____

By the Book

Al and his friends want to grow lots of vegetables this summer, so they got a book on gardening. Here's a copy of the book's index. Use it to figure out what page(s) they should check to find the answer to each question below.

Something Extra

Look at your own books or some in the library. Choose one topic that you'd like to know more about. Then use the index to find out where to read about that topic.

1. How do I plant tomatoes? _____

2. When can I harvest my beans? _____

3. Are Japanese beetles a garden pest? _____

4. What do I use a trowel for? _____

5. What tools do I need for my garden? _____

6. How often should I water the garden? _____

7. What insects are bad for plants? _____

8. What can I use compost for? _____

9. Where can I get seed catalogs? _____

10. What diseases do plants get? _____

Beans, 9, 20
Beets, 11, 21
Broccoli, 10, 20
Carrots, 7, 19
Catalogs, seed, 4
Compost
    making a compost pile, 27
    using compost, 28
Cucumbers, 12, 21
Diseases, plant, 29
Fertilizers, 26
Green beans. See beans.

Harvesting
  beans, 20
  beets, 21
  broccoli, 20
  carrots, 19
  cucumbers, 21
  lettuce, 19
  tomatoes, 22
Insects
  hornworms, 30
  Japanese beetles, 31
  pests, 30-31

Lettuce, 8, 19
Planning, garden, 2-3
Seeds, 4, 7-15
Tomatoes, 13, 22
Tools, garden, 5-6
  rake, 5
  trowel, 6
Watering, 25

Good Guys, Bad Guys

Read each sentence below and think about what it says. Then decide if the boldfaced creature is a garden "good guy" or a garden "bad guy." Put a check mark in the column to show what you think.

Something Extra

Go on a bug hunt. You can find bugs anywhere—in your garden, backyard, a park—even in your basement! Count the different kinds you find. You'll be amazed at how many there are!

An **earthworm** digs tunnels that let water and air get into the soil.

Aphids suck all the juice from plants.

A **cutworm** can chew right through a plant's stem.

An **earwig** eats flower petals and soft leaves.

A **honeybee** carries pollen from one plant to another.

A **hornworm** loves to munch on tomato leaves.

A **Japanese beetle** eats flowers and leaves.

A **ladybug** eats aphids and other insect pests.

A **slug** lunches on tender seedlings.

A **spider** catches plant-eating insects in its web.

A **toad** eats caterpillars and other insects that kill plants.

Good Guy	Bad Guy

Did You Know?

Insects are the largest animal family of all. More than 800,000 different kinds of insects have been identified by scientists. And insects have been around for a long time, too. There are some insect fossils that are more than 400 million years old!

Drawing Conclusions

Swim Time

Summer and swimming go together. It doesn't matter if you swim in a pool, a lake, or the ocean—getting wet is a great way to cool down! So it's a good idea to know how to swim—and that means taking lessons.

Read the schedule below. Then write each kid's name under the clock that shows the time of his or her lesson.

Something Extra

See if you can find a stopwatch to borrow. Then work with a friend to time yourselves doing something. How fast can you run around the block? How long can you hold your breath? How far can you swim in 30 seconds?

Private Swim Lesson Schedule

Tori	8:20	Al	10:15
Eddie	8:50	Tanesha	11:05
Sung	9:25	Kelsey	11:40
Matt	9:45	Ben	12:10

Did You Know?

People love the idea of swimming the English Channel—a distance of 21 miles. The first person to swim the channel was Matthew Webb of England. The trip took him almost 22 hours, and he used the breast stroke the whole time.

Plural Endings

Plural means more than one person, place, or thing.
Most singular nouns can be made plural by adding **s**.

Write each word. Add **s**.

1. flower _____

2. sister _____

3. bird _____

4. toy _____

When a word ends in **x**, **ss**, **ch**, or **sh**, add **es**.

5. box _____

6. bench _____

7. dress _____

8. tax _____

For most nouns that end with a consonant **y**, change
the **y** to **i** and add **es**.

9. puppy _____

10. berry _____

11. city _____

12. story _____

Write each word from the word box
with the correct plural ending.

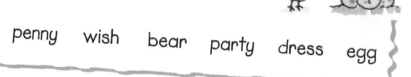

penny   wish   bear   party   dress   egg

_____   _____

_____   _____

_____   _____

Independence Day

The Fourth of July is America's birthday. So this year, remember to say, "Happy Birthday, America!"

In 1774, many colonists were unhappy with England. They did not like paying taxes when they had no say in running the colonies. So a group of colonists formed the First Continental Congress.

Then, in April 1775, the British army marched toward Concord, Massachusetts. They wanted to take away the weapons the colonists were storing there.

A group of citizen-soldiers, the minutemen, blocked the British troops. This was the first battle of the American Revolution.

In May, there was a Second Continental Congress. In June, this group wrote a document that said the colonies were independent of England.

On July 4, 1776, the Declaration of Independence was signed. A new nation—the United States of America—was born.

What does the word *independence* mean to you?

_____

_____

What if the English king had allowed the colonists to run their own government? Or what if he had stopped making the colonies pay taxes? Do you think the American Revolution would have happened? Why or why not?

_____

_____

_____

_____

Fireworks Words

Adjectives and adverbs are the "fireworks" in sentences. They make sentences interesting because they describe how things look and happen. **Adjectives** are words that tell about nouns. **Adverbs** are words that tell about verbs.

Read the sentences below. Circle each adjective. Draw a line under each adverb. Remember that adverbs often end in -ly, but not always!

1. The colorful float moved quickly.

2. A huge crowd of people watched happily.

3. The marching band played a merry tune.

4. The hot sun made everyone move slowly.

5. A striped flag waved wildly from a brick building

6. The thirsty kids bought cold drinks.

7. Everyone sat comfortably on the soft grass.

8. Bright fireworks soared high into the inky sky.

9. A small child cried when the fireworks exploded loudly.

10. A cool shower made the fireworks end suddenly.

Did You Know?

Adjectives usually describe nouns—words that name persons, places, or things. But sometimes an adjective and noun seem odd used together because they have meanings that are almost opposites. These combinations are called oxymorons. Here are a few examples: bad health, old news, jumbo shrimp, genuine imitation, and least favorite.

Math Blast!

Have a Fourth of July blast solving these subtraction problems. Be careful—you may have to regroup. Write the answer under each problem. Then write the letter for each solution at the bottom of the page in order from the lowest to the highest.

U 456
−136
☐

T 645
−207
☐

H 607
− 29
☐

A 234
−148
☐

Y 560
−399
☐

P 389
−299
☐

R 611
−209
☐

O 491
−199
☐

H 428
−388
☐

F 435
−256
☐

P 480
−345
☐

Here is your holiday greeting!

___ ___ ___ ___

___ ___ ___ ___ ___ ___ ___ !

What Goes Up...

Gravity is a force of attraction between two objects. Large, heavy objects have stronger pull than smaller objects. The earth's gravity pulls everything toward the center of the planet. That's what keeps people and buildings from sailing off into outer space!

Look at the Fourth of July picnic scene. Put an **X** on everything that shows gravity at work. Find at least eight examples.

LAUGH LINES

Can you find the center of gravity?

It's the letter v!

Sandwich Search

Al made himself lunch, but when he put it down on the picnic table, it got mixed up with everyone else's. Read the clues. Then circle Al's lunch.

Al loves grapes.
He prefers turkey to ham.
He doesn't like tomatoes on his sandwich.
Al always uses whole wheat bread for sandwiches.
He doesn't like celery.

Something Extra

Ask if you can make a layered sandwich for lunch. Get creative! Make layers of green or red pepper, onion, zucchini or summer squash, carrots, tomatoes, mushrooms—anything you like.

Did You Know?

According to legend, the sandwich was invented by a British lord—the Earl of Sandwich. One day the earl didn't want to stop what he was doing to eat lunch. He told a servant to just put some meat between two slices of bread and bring it to him. The sandwich was born!

Insect Alert

Everything that creeps, flies, and crawls around the picnic table isn't an insect. Adult insects have special characteristics that are different from birds, reptiles, amphibians, and mammals.

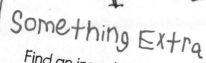

Something Extra

Find an insect. Can you identify all the body parts? If not, maybe it isn't an insect. Or maybe it's not an adult. A caterpillar doesn't have legs or wings, but it is an insect. When it's an adult, it will be a moth or butterfly—complete with wings and six legs.

To be an insect, an animal must have these characteristics.

- Three body parts—a head, a thorax, and an abdomen.
- Wings—most have one pair of wings or two. Wings can be hard like a beetle's, or soft like a mosquito's. Wings are attached to the thorax.
- Six legs—also attached to the thorax.
- Antennae
- Eyes
- Mouthparts for biting, sucking, sipping, or lapping up food.

Look at the grasshopper below. Can you label all its parts?

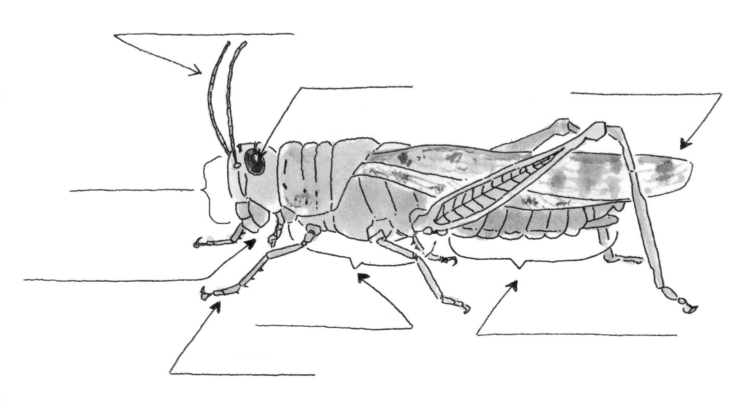

Shell Patterns

The kids found lots of shells when they went beachcombing.

conch  mussel  scallop  limpet snail

Look at how the shells are arranged and think about the pattern in each row. Write the name of the shell that comes next.

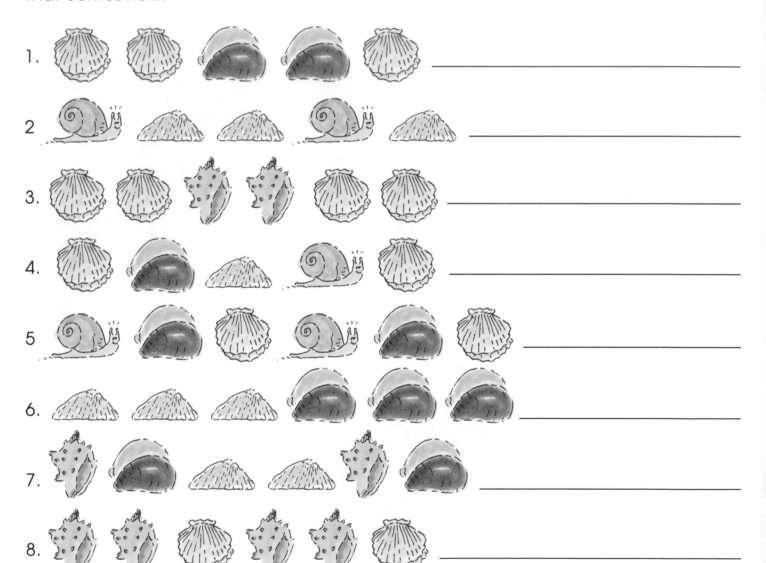

1. _____

2 _____

3. _____

4. _____

5 _____

6. _____

7. _____

8. _____

Litter Picker

Make a summertime promise to be a litter-picker. Don't leave anything behind when you go to the beach or on a picnic. Take your trash home and recycle whatever you can.

Look at the litter left on the beach! Think about the material used to make each item. Write the number of products that belong in each recycling bin.

Sandy Synonyms

Read the sentences below. If the blue word is new to you, think about the sentence to get a clue about what the word means. Then look on the shells to find a **synonym** for the word—a word with almost the same meaning. Write the number of the sentence on the shell that has the correct synonym.

Something Extra
Antonyms are words that have opposite meanings. For example, hot and cold are antonyms. (So are antonym and synonym!) Can you think of antonyms for forlorn, grasped, and gingerly?

1. It was a hot day, and there were hordes of people at the beach.
2. Kelsey sat and gazed out at the water.
3. Al held an angry crab gingerly.
4. Tori grasped her bucket in both hands to keep it from floating away.
5. Water came through a gap in the walls of the sandcastle.
6. The kids couldn't prevent the tide from coming in.
7. The sharp shells were a hazard to bare feet.
8. Tori was forlorn when her wonderful day at the beach was over.

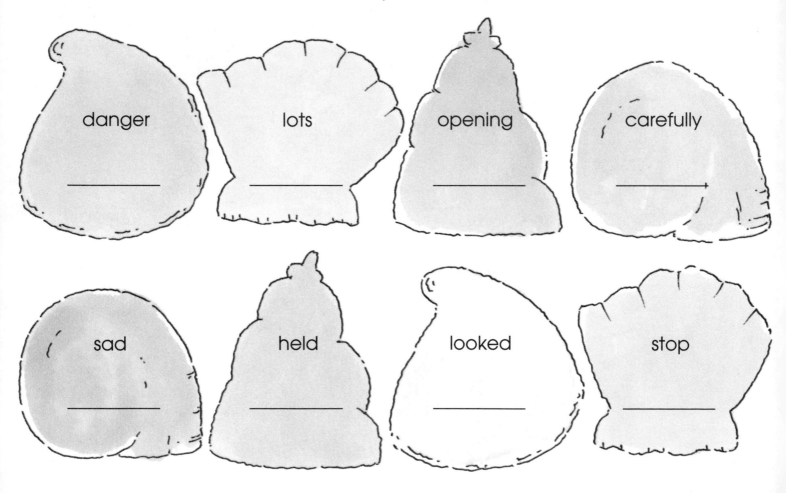

danger _____

lots _____

opening _____

carefully _____

sad _____

held _____

looked _____

stop _____

Three-Scoop Addition

There's nothing like an ice cream cone to lick the heat. You can lick these three-scoop addition problems, too. Add the numbers and write the sum on the cone. Don't forget to regroup.

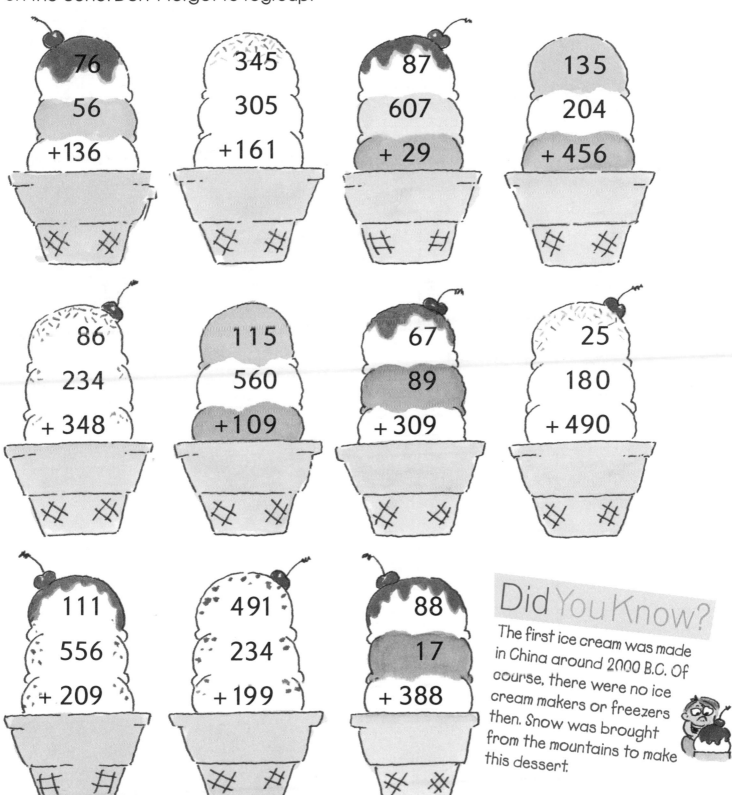

```
   76        345        87        135
   56        305       607        204
 +136       +161      + 29      + 456
```

```
   86        115        67         25
  234        560        89        180
 + 348      +109      + 309      + 490
```

```
  111        491        88
  556        234        17
 + 209      +199      + 388
```

Map Mania

The kids are excited because their summer swim team is headed for Illinois to compete in a big swim meet. But they aren't all sure exactly where Illinois is, so they took out a map to find it.

Use the map to complete the table below. Start in the middle of each state listed in the first column. Then move in the direction listed in the second column. In the last column, write the name of the state in which you end up. Don't get lost!

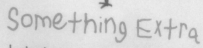

Something Extra

Label your state by putting a big X on the map to show where you live. Where would you end up if you traveled north? south? east? west?

Start in	Head	End up in
Illinois	east	
Pennsylvania	north	
Maine	southwest	
South Dakota	south	
Nevada	west	
Delaware	north	
Oklahoma	south	
Mississippi	northwest	
Florida	northwest	
Colorado	west	
Minnesota	east	
Connecticut	north	
West Virginia	northwest	
Oregon	east	

© 2000 School Zone Publishing Company

Did You Know?

There are different kinds of maps. Two common kinds are political and physical maps. Political maps show countries, states, provinces, cities, towns—ways humans have divided up the land. Physical maps show what the surface of the earth is like—how high or low the land is, where lakes and rivers are located, and so on.

Movie Night

Tori, Al, and Kelsey are going to the movies. They each have $12.00 to spend. Tickets cost $5.25 each. Refreshments are extra.

Check the price list. Then figure out how much each kid spends and how much change he or she has left.

	SMALL	MEDIUM	LARGE
Popcorn	1.50	2.50	3.00
Soda	1.50		2.50
Licorice	2.00		
Gumdrops	2.00		

Tori

ticket $ ____ . ____

small popcorn   ____ . ____

small soda   ____ . ____ $ ____ . ____

gumdrops   ____ . ____

                $ ____ . ____ $ ____ . ____ $ _____ . ____

Tori's change

Al

ticket $ ____ . ____

licorice   ____ . ____

gumdrops   ____ . ____ $ ____ . ____

large soda   ____ . ____   ____ . ____

                $ ____ . ____ $ ____ . ____ $ _____ . ____

Al's change

Kelsey

ticket $ ____ . ____

small popcorn   ____ . ____ $ ____ . ____

large soda   ____ . ____   ____ . ____

                $ ____ . ____ $ ____ . ____ $ _____ . ____

Kelsey's change

Addition and Subtraction (Dollars and Cents)   © 2000 School Zone Publishing Company

Making Sense

To make sense of your surroundings, you need to use your senses. Everything you see, hear, taste, touch, and smell gives you important information.

Read the sentences below. Which of the five senses is being used **most** in each example?

1. "Ugh! I think there's gum under my seat," Tori said.
2. Al chewed on a red gumdrop.
3. One whiff of Tori's popcorn made Kelsey decide to buy some, too.
4. "The star of the movie has short hair now," commented Al.
5. Tori didn't like the loud music at the beginning of the movie.
6. Al ducked when a spaceship came toward him on the screen.
7. Kelsey hummed along with the movie's theme song.
8. During a scary part, Tori grabbed Kelsey's arm.
9. When Al unwrapped his gumdrops, Kelsey became hungry.
10. Tori licked the butter off her fingers.

Write the sentence number under the correct heading.

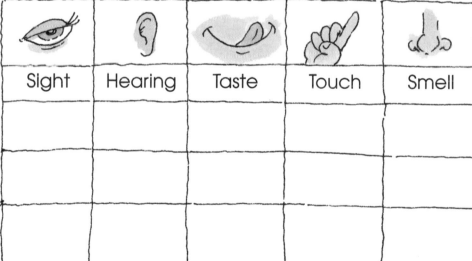

Sight	Hearing	Taste	Touch	Smell

Did You Know?

Mammals have the best hearing of any animals. But even though humans are mammals, we aren't near the top of the list for good hearing. Most animals hear much better than humans do. They might be better listeners, too!

Heading Downtown

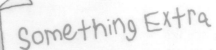

Matt, Al, Tori, and Kelsey are heading downtown to explore the city. The timetable shows the schedule for buses that go from Brewster Street to downtown. Use the timetable to answer the questions below.

Something Extra

Find a timetable for buses, planes, trains, ferryboats, or some other form of transportation. Make up some questions that can be answered by the timetable. Or use the timetable to schedule a trip that your family plans to make.

Daily Schedule	Brewster Street		Eastside Mall		Downtown
	Arrival	Departure	Arrival	Departure	Arrival
Bus #23	7:02 A.M.	7:07 A.M.	7:25 A.M.	7:40 A.M.	8:01 A.M.
Bus #45	7:32 A.M.	7:37 A.M.			8:26 A.M.
Bus #127	8:32 A.M.	8:37 A.M.	8:55 A.M.	9:10 A.M.	9:31 A.M.
Bus #23	10:47 A.M.	10:52 A.M.	11:10 A.M.	11:25 A.M.	11:46 A.M.
Bus #127	3:56 P.M.	4:01 P.M.	4:19 P.M.	4:34 P.M.	4:55 P.M.
Bus #23	4:30 P.M.	4:35 P.M.	4:53 P.M.	5:08 P.M.	5:29 P.M.
Bus #45	5:06 P.M.	5:11 P.M.			6:00 P.M.
Bus #127	6:06 P.M.	6:11 P.M.	6:29 P.M.	6:44 P.M.	7:05 P.M.

1. If you want to go from Brewster Street to downtown without stopping, which bus should you take? _____ What time does it leave Brewster Street? _____

2. How long does Bus #23 wait at Brewster Street before leaving? _____

3. How long does it take Bus #127 to get downtown from the time it arrives at Brewster Street? _____

4. How long does Bus #45 take to get downtown when it doesn't stop at Eastside Mall? _____

5. If you have to get downtown before 9:00 A.M., which two buses could you take?

   (Give the bus number and time.) _____ or _____

Downtown Vowels

Kelsey, Tori, Matt, and Al are ready to head home after their trip downtown. But they're having some trouble with a tricky vowel sound. Read the paragraph below. Each word with missing letters has the same vowel sound you hear in "downtown." Decide whether the sound should be spelled *ow* or *ou*.

"Let's get on the bus right n __ __," said Kelsey in a l __ __ d voice.

Al laughed. "Calm d __ __ n, Kelsey. It doesn't leave for another five minutes."

Tori spoke up. "If we wait, the bus will be too cr __ __ ded." Matt said, "Okay, okay.

Let's get on." They all sat d __ __ n and started to talk about their day.

"H __ __ did you like going up to the top of the bank building?" asked Kelsey.

"I felt like we were up in the cl __ __ ds when we got to the top!" said Matt.

"The best part of the day was the clam ch __ __ der we ate for lunch," said Al.

"I thought the best thing was the f __ __ ntain," commented Matt.

"There were more coins in there than I could c __ __ nt!" Al exclaimed.

Did You Know?

English can be a very confusing language. Just think about these words: dough, rough, cough, through. They all have the same four letters at the end—yet none of them rhyme!

Out on a Limb!

A family tree shows the people who make up your family. Family trees can include all kinds of relatives—from cousins to grandparents to great-aunts and uncles. Or they can be simple and just show parents and grandparents.

Tori made this family tree before going to her family reunion. Use it to answer the questions.

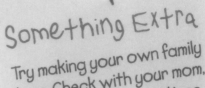

Something Extra
Try making your own family tree. Check with your mom, dad, and older relatives for information about who to include.

1. What relationship is Angelo Rinaldi to Tori? _____

2. Who did Michael Grady marry? _____

3. What was the name of the son of George and Eleanor James?

   _____

4. What is his relationship to Tori? _____

5. Who is Tori probably named for? (Hint: Tori is a nickname.)

   _____

6. How many of Tori's great-grandparents are still living?

   _____

7. Who is Tori's oldest living relative? _____

8. What is the name of Tori's mother's father? _____

9. What is the name of Victoria Reiser's father? _____

10. Who is Tori's oldest grandmother? _____

Frederick James
b. 1915; d. 1944

Margaret Wilson
b. 1916; d. 1998

Michael Grady
b. 1910; d. 1985

Anna O'Toole
b. 1916

Joshua Reiser
b. 1920; d. 1987

Elizabeth Warren
b. 1921

Angelo Rinaldi
b. 1915; d. 1999

Maria Catalo
b. 1916; d. 1990

George James
b. 1935

Eleanor Grady
b. 1935

Victoria Reiser
b. 1942

Joseph Rinaldi
b. 1942

Fred James
b. 1966

Margery Rinaldi
b. 1968

Tori James

Fun in the ~~Son~~ Sun

(HI SON!)

Tori just arrived at her family's reunion. She's happy to see everyone, but she isn't sure if she's saying hello to her aunt or her ant. That's because Tori has trouble with homophones—words that sound the same but have different spellings and different meanings. Of course, you know that Tori is talking to her aunt—because an ant is an insect!

Choose the correct word for each sentence.

1. Tori knew she would have a _____ time.   **grate great**

2. Everyone was happy that the _____ was good.   **weather whether**

3. The picnic tables sat in a grove of _____ trees.   **fir fur**

4. Grandpa couldn't believe how much Tori had _____.   **groan grown**

5. The park had a lake with a sandy _____.   **beech beach**

6. Everyone ran around in _____ feet.   **bare bear**

7. At noon, Dad put the _____ on the grill.   **meet meat**

8. For _____, grandma brought two apple pies.   **desert dessert**

9. Uncle Willy _____ four pieces of pie!   **ate eight**

10. At night, it started to get a little _____.   **chilly chili**

11. The children were _____ to stay up late.   **aloud allowed**

12. Tori talked so much that the next day she was _____.   **horse hoarse**

A Piece O' Pie

Everyone enjoyed the pies at Tori's family reunion. But there were so many pies that there were leftovers. Look at the fractions written under each pie. Circle the fraction that shows how much of the pie is left over—the part that has NOT been eaten.

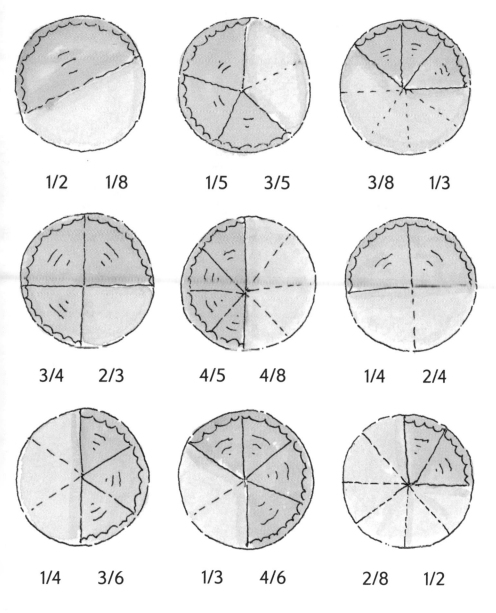

1/2   1/8   1/5   3/5   3/8   1/3

3/4   2/3   4/5   4/8   1/4   2/4

1/4   3/6   1/3   4/6   2/8   1/2

Sometimes different fractions equal the same thing. Find each picture that shows one-half of a pie left over. How many different ways is 1/2 shown? Write each leftover pie fraction that equals 1/2 on the line.

_____

LAUGH LINES

What's the best thing to put into a pie?

Your teeth!

Camp Mos-Kee-Toe

A map gives you a kind of picture of an area as if you were seeing it from above. Maps use colors, lines, and symbols to show where things are located. The map key tells you what these things mean.

The map below shows part of Camp Mos-Kee-Toe. Study the map to circle the best answer for each question.

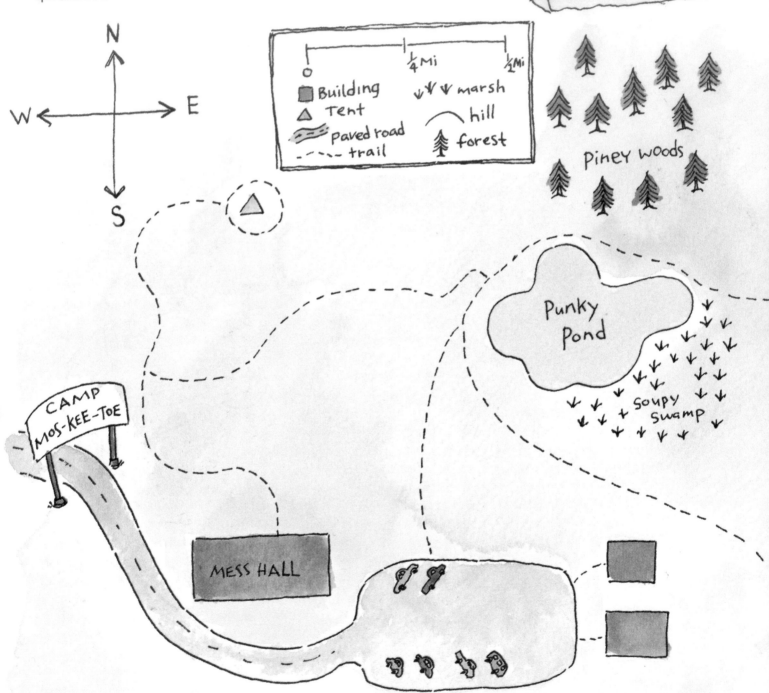

1. The campers' tents are _____ of the Mess Hall.
   east   south   north

2. About how long is the trail from the northern edge of Punky Pond to the Mess Hall?
   5 miles   2 miles   1/2 mile

3. Soupy Swamp is on the _____ side of Punky Pond.
   southeast   northeast   southwest

4. The entrance to Camp Mos-Kee-Toe is at the _____ corner of the camp.
   northeast   northwest   southwest

5. Which direction are the Piney Woods from the tents?
   east   south   southwest

6. If a hiker takes the trail from the parking lot and always stays
   to the right, where will he or she finally end up?
   Catfish Lake   Punky Pond   Piney Woods

7. Which camp location can be reached by car?
   tents   Mess Hall   Piney Woods

8. About how long is the trail from Catfish Lake to the
   parking lot?
   10 miles   40 miles   3 miles

CATFISH LAKE

CREEK

WISHY WASHY

Did You Know?

People have been making maps for centuries. The first known map was created in the sixth century B.C. by a Greek philosopher. It only showed the world as it was known to Greeks at that time. So Greece was in the center of the map surrounded by ocean.

Camp Quotes

Something Extra
Pick one of your favorite newspaper comic strips and rewrite the words in sentence form.

It's strange but true—thinking about comic strips can help you write quotations correctly! Imagine that the quotation marks take the place of the cartoon balloon. Everything inside the balloon goes inside quotation marks—including the punctuation.

Try this trick out by writing each kid's comments as a sentence that uses quotation marks. Use a comma to separate the speaker's name from what he or she is saying. One example is done for you.

1. Al asked, "Which way is the lake?"
   _____

2. _____

3. _____

4. _____

5. _____

6. _____

7. _____

8. _____

WHICH WAY IS THE LAKE?

I CAN'T WAIT TO GO SWIMMING!

2.

1.

AL

KELLY

LAKE

Writing Dialogue (Quotation Marks)

Writing Dialogue (Quotation Marks)

Going Buggy

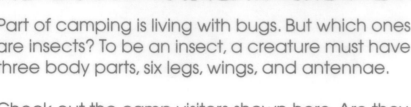

Something Extra

Look at each creature that you decided is not an insect. Tell why you made that decision.

Part of camping is living with bugs. But which ones are insects? To be an insect, a creature must have three body parts, six legs, wings, and antennae.

Check out the camp visitors shown here. Are they insects or not? Circle *yes* or *no*.

YES   NO

YES   NO

YES   NO

YES   NO

YES   NO

YES   NO

YES   NO

YES   NO

YES   NO

YES   NO

YES   NO

YES   NO

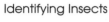

Nature Notes

Naturalists are scientists who study nature. Like all scientists, they keep careful records of what they observe. Their records include words, sketches, maps, and more.

Anyone can be a naturalist. There is plenty to see at the beach, in a park, beside a stream—even in your own backyard!

Head out to find something to study—an ant, a frog, a bird, a plant—anything that interests you. Then record what you see. Include some sketches and a map that shows where you did your observing.

Butterfly on Dandelion

Milk weed Seed

Bird nest with eggs

Eggs are blue with dark speckles

probably robin's

found in small tree

near edge of woods

egg

Beetle

American Toad

Frogs and Toads each start their lives as Tadpoles.

Tadpole

Did You Know?

John James Audubon was a naturalist in the early 1800s. He is best known for his wildlife paintings—especially of birds. In 1838 his book *The Birds of America* was published. It has illustrations of over 1,000 birds. The National Audubon Society was named in honor of Audubon.

At the Fair

It's time for the fair! Everyone is excited about seeing the animals, riding the roller coaster and Ferris wheel, and eating cotton candy and saltwater taffy.

The number of people who attended the fair each day is shown.

Something Extra

Check your newspaper for information about attendance at a fair or sporting event. Write the figure in words instead of numerals.

1. The day that it rained had the lowest attendance. Which day did it rain?

   _____

2. The highest attendance is always on the day of the fireworks. Which day was the fireworks display?

   _____

3. Which day had higher attendance, Friday or Sunday?

   _____

4. How many people attended the fair on Saturday and Sunday combined?

   _____

5. How many more people attended the fair on Saturday than on Tuesday?

   _____

The Complete Story

To be complete, a sentence must have a **subject** (who or what the sentence is about) and a **predicate** (what the subject does or experiences).

Read each numbered example below. If it is a complete sentence, make a slash between the subject and predicate and write OK on the line. If it is NOT a complete sentence, make it one by adding a subject or predicate. Then write the complete sentence on the line.

1. The fair started on Monday afternoon. _____

2. Were in stalls in the barn. _____

3. The Ferris wheel is 40 feet tall. _____

4. Kelsey's mother won a blue ribbon. _____

5. The entrance booth. _____

6. An all-day ticket. _____

7. Al bought cotton candy. _____

Did You Know?

Pronouns are words that take the place of nouns. So a pronoun can be the subject of a sentence. Each pronoun below is the subject of its sentence.

He ran across the street.
They sat on the beach.
It sailed up into the sky.

What's the Matter?

Matter is anything that takes up space. Matter is found in three different forms—solids, liquids, and gases. A solid has a definite shape. It doesn't change its shape unless forced to. A liquid can flow and take the shape of its container. A gas has no definite size or shape. It can spread out to fit any size container.

Look at the backyard scene. Then list two things under each form of matter.

LiQuid	GAS	SoLiD

Make Lemonade!

Nothing tastes better on a hot summer day than a cold glass of lemonade. A lemonade stand is a great way to make money in the summer!

LEMONADE 10¢

Luscious Lemonade

In a large pitcher, combine these ingredients:

12 cups water
4 cups lemon juice
2 cups sugar

Stir until the sugar dissolves. Makes one gallon of lemonade.

Note: 4 fresh lemons = 1 cup lemon juice

1 tablespoon = 3 teaspoons
1 cup = 16 tablespoons
1 pint = 2 cups
1 quart = 4 cups
1 gallon = 4 quarts

1. Write the amount of each ingredient needed to make one-half gallon of lemonade.

   _____ cups water

   _____ cups lemon juice

   _____ cup sugar

2. How many quarts of water and lemon juice does it take to make one gallon of lemonade?

   _____

3. How many fresh lemons do you need to make one gallon of lemonade?

4. Fresh lemons cost $0.25 each. A quart of bottled lemon juice costs $2.40. Which would be cheaper to use when making lemonade?

The Water Cycle

Summer weather is very changeable. A sunny day can quickly turn into a cloudy one. Clouds often mean rain—or even a thunderstorm. Rain is one way water moves through the water cycle.

The sentences on the next page describe the water cycle. Number the boxes to show which part of the water cycle is described by each sentence.

POROUS EARTH

GROUND WATER

1. The sun shines on the earth and heats the water.
2. Heated water evaporates, becomes water vapor, and rises into the air.
3. The wind blows the air toward land.
4. Hills and mountains force the air to rise.
5. As the air rises, it cools and condenses, forming clouds.
6. Water falls from clouds as precipitation—rain, snow, hail, or sleet.
7. Plants and animals use some of the water.
8. Some water goes into the ground and begins to flow back to the ocean.
9. Water from lakes, ponds, rivers, and streams flows back to the ocean.

Holiday Hoopla

In the United States, Flag Day is celebrated in June, Independence Day in July, and Labor Day in September. Each holiday has its own customs and symbols, such as flag displays, fireworks, and parades. But poor August has no national holiday. Invent your own August holiday. It can be a day in honor of anything you want to celebrate!

Name of holiday: _____

Date: _____

Reason for celebration: _____

_____

_____

Special holiday events: _____

_____

_____

Holiday symbol: _____

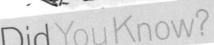

Did You Know?

Summer has plenty of celebrations. A few are Midsummer's Day in Finland and Great Britain; Bastille Day in France; the Feast of Fortune in Japan; and Independence Day in more than a dozen countries!

Cool Comparisons

An **analogy** is a statement that compares two sets of words, and shows how they go together. For example, butterfly is to insect as rabbit is to mammal. Both sets of words name an animal and the family it belongs to.

Each summertime analogy below is missing one word. Figure out how the first two words in each set go together. Then write a "cool" word to finish the analogy.

berries	waves	water
hills	cold	noisemakers
night	rake	cats	school

1. Summer is to hot as winter is to _____.

2. Ice cream is to milk as jelly is to _____.

3. Swimming is to water as hiking is to _____.

4. Parks are to trees as lakes are to _____.

5. Breeze is to wind as ripples are to _____.

6. Grass is to mow as leaves are to _____.

7. Sunshine is to day as moonlight is to _____.

8. Mosquitoes are to ants as dogs are to _____.

9. July is to fireworks as January is to _____.

10. Picnic is to park as study is to _____.

Then and Now

Historical villages show what life was like long ago. Al had a fun visit to one. Now he's grateful for modern things like air conditioning and swimming pools.

Take a walk through this historical village. Look at each set of pictures. Put an **X** through the item in each set that is too modern to be on display in the village.

Something Extra

Look around your house. Can you find three things that might have been in a home 100 years ago? Can you find three things that would never have been found in a home 100 years ago?

WELCOME TO OLD TOWN EST. ____

Did You Know?

Most historical villages are made up of buildings that have been moved to a new location. But if you visit Williamsburg, Virginia, you can walk on the exact same street that George Washington did, and sit on a bench where Thomas Jefferson sat. The buildings have been where they are since the town was founded.

Quilt Geometry

Historical villages often have old quilts on display. Many quilts are made up of blocks that have geometric patterns.

Look at the two quilt blocks below. How many triangles can you find in the first block? How many squares can you find in the second? Don't be fooled—some shapes overlap.

Something Extra

Design a quilt block on paper using triangles, squares, and rectangles. Then color it in to show a pattern.

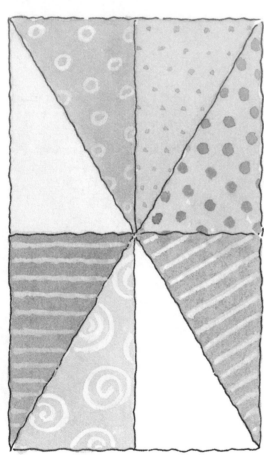

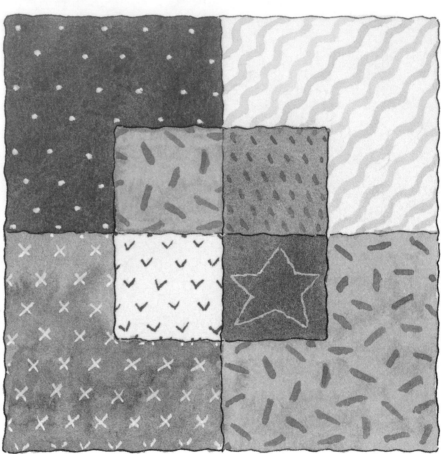

_____ triangles

_____ squares

Did You Know?

When people made quilts long ago, they weren't just thinking of creating something beautiful. They were being careful not to waste anything. Most quilts were made of bits and pieces of leftover fabric and scraps cut from clothing that had worn out.

In the Swim

It's time for a swim meet! As usual, the fastest time wins. Add up the numbers in each lane to see who swims the length of the pool in the fewest minutes. Remember to do the work in each set of parentheses ( ) first. Write each swimmer's time on the lines.

SERF'S UP!

Something Extra

Try writing a long math problem for someone else to solve. Use parentheses to separate each step of the problem. But be careful—make sure you know the answer!

1. $(12 - 6) - (3 \times 2) + (10 \div 10) + (6 - 2) =$ _____

2. $(14 - 7) + (2 \times 2) - (3 \times 1) - (6 - 0) =$ _____

3. $(9 + 5) + (5 \times 0) - (15 \div 5) - (3 + 4) =$ _____

4. $(6 - 5) - (3 \times 0) + (6 + 6) - (2 \times 5) =$ _____

5. $(12 - 9) + (3 \times 3) + (5 \times 0) - (3 + 1) =$ _____

6. $(4 \div 4) + (6 \times 3) - (5 + 5) + (1 - 0) =$ _____

7. $(8 + 4) - (4 \times 2) + (2 \times 4) - (2 \times 3) =$ _____

8. $(3 \times 1) - (2 \times 1) + (1 \times 4) - (1 \times 2) =$ _____

Did You Know?

During the Middle Ages, swimming was not popular. People believed that sickness could be spread by water. Even baths were thought to be dangerous!

Celebration Cinquain

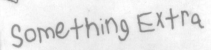

It's been a great summer! Celebrate it by writing a **cinquain** about summer. A cinquain is a simple, five-line poem that doesn't rhyme. The pattern of the poem looks like this:

Something Extra

Try writing another unrhymed poem—a haiku. The haiku is a Japanese poem that usually has to do with nature. Haiku have three lines. Line one has five syllables, line two has seven syllables, and line three has five syllables.

Line 1: a two-syllable word that names the subject of the poem

Line 2: four syllables that describe the subject

Line 3: six syllables that show action

Line 4: eight syllables that tell more about the subject

Line 5: two syllables that rename or sum up the subject

Write a cinquain about summer. The first line is done for you!

Summer
_____

_____

_____

_____

Summer—

Do you have the time?

Midnight!

Did You Know?

If you really want to celebrate long summer days, you should live in Hammerfest, Norway. From May 14 until July 30, the sun never sets! There is a disadvantage to living there, however. From the middle of November until the end of January, the sun never rises.

Mailbag

It's exciting to open the mailbox and find a letter addressed to you. The best way to get mail is to send some yourself.

Write to a friend or family member who lives in another town, state, or country. Be sure to include all the parts of a friendly letter. Tell him or her about what you have been doing during the summer. Maybe you will get a letter in reply!

Date

July 5, 2000

Greeting

Dear Ms. Jones,

Body

Thank you very much for letting us visit Green Gardens. We enjoyed learning about plants in the indoor and outdoor gardens. We had fun collecting different kinds of leaves. We especially loved watching the baby quail run around.

Best wishes, **Closing**

Mrs. Cone's class

Signature

Categorize

Matt is shopping for school supplies, but somehow his lists got mixed up.

Look at the items on each store list. Cross out the thing that doesn't belong. Add it to the list where it most likely will be found. When you get done, Matt should have four things to buy at each store.

Something Extra

Make a list of back-to-school supplies that you need. Just be sure you don't end up with a mixed-up mess like Matt did!

GOOD TIME GROCERY

Slippers
Pretzels
Bread
Peanut Butter

CARL'S Clothing Store

Shorts
Socks
T-Shirt
Pencils

OFFICE SUPPLY STORE

Crayons
Paper
Gym bag
Ruler

SPORTS STORE

Basketball
Backpack
Apples
Baseball

VILLAGE SHOE STORE

Sandals
Blue Jeans
Sneakers
Boots

Language Arts Activities to Share

Summer is a perfect time to share a good book with your child. Try new favorites like the Harry Potter books by J.K. Rowling. Add in classics such as *Charlotte's Web* by E.B. White, *The Wind in the Willows* by Kenneth Grahame, *Charlie and the Chocolate Factory* by Roald Dahl, and any of Shel Silverstein's poetry books. Some helpful references for ideas about reading together are *50 Simple Things You Can Do to Raise a Child Who Loves to Read* by Kathy A. Zahler and *The New York Times Parent's Guide to the Best Books for Children* by Eden Ross Lipson. Another good reference for parents is *The Right Start to Teach Your Child to Read* by Jim Hoffman.

Play with Words Have some fun with palindromes and anagrams. Palindromes are words that are spelled the same forward and backward. See how many the family can list. Here are examples: dad, mom, noon, peep, eye, and gag. Anagrams are words that are formed from the letters of another word. For example, sear is an anagram for ears. Some other anagram pairs are read and dear; plug and gulp; guns and snug; bag and gab.

Look It Up Take a trip to the local library to help your child research a topic of interest. Check each book's index to find the topic. Use the library's encyclopedias. Go on-line at the library—or at home—to find information. A great search engine for kids is www.yahooligans.com

Think about It Build creativity by stretching your child's mind. Ask questions like the following: How many uses can you think of for a sock? a safety pin? a brick? How are a box and a book alike? a pumpkin and a pizza? Have fun—there are no right or wrong answers!

Word Power Build your child's vocabulary by choosing a Word of the Day each day of the summer. Introduce the word and its meaning. Then try to use it throughout the day. Choose words that are fun and impressive to say, like gargantuan, neophyte, and plethora.

Summer Playhouse Encourage your child to set up a summer playhouse with friends. Let kids act out stories with costumes, props, tickets, and an audience. Their stage can be the basement, garage, front porch, deck, or yard.

See the Movie Read a book together and then rent the video. Talk about how the book and video are alike and different and which version you each prefer. Some suggestions include *The Red Balloon, Charlie and the Chocolate Factory* (video title: *Willy Wonka and the Chocolate Factory*), *Alice in Wonderland, The Jungle Book, James and the Giant Peach, Peter Pan, The Black Cauldron,* and *The Wizard of Oz*.

Get Ready Prepare your child for a new school year with School Zone's *Language Arts 2* and *Language Arts 3-4*. These deluxe edition workbooks are colorful, affordable, and filled with fun activities.

Math Activities to Share

The National Council of Teachers of Mathematics (NCTM) recommends that children have hands-on, varied math experiences using manipulatives, calculators, and computers. The NCTM stresses having children "make sense" of math by connecting it to real life. You can help your child accomplish the NCTM goals with activities such as the following.

Food Fractions Follow up on the fraction activity in this book by turning a snack into fun with fractions. Graham crackers work well for showing parts of a whole. Talk about the fractions as you snack—for example, "Let's eat 1/2 of a graham cracker now." Use crackers to practice identifying fractional parts of a group. Hand out 12 crackers; then identify how many represent 1/2, 1/3, or 1/6 of the total. This is a great way to practice division skills, too.

Math Riddles Play mental math games while riding in the car to a summertime destination. Ask your child to solve riddles such as the following: "You have two turtles, three pigeons, and a horse. How many legs in all?"

Make Math Fun Check out a great math book. Examples include *I Hate Mathematics!* and *Math for Smarty Pants,* both by Marilyn Burns. The books are filled with fun—and funny—hands-on activities that reinforce math concepts.

Make Lemonade Let your child use the recipe found in this book to make lemonade. Following the recipe gives hands-on practice with measuring volume. And if your child actually sets up a lemonade stand in the neighborhood, he or she can practice working with money as well!

Solve Problems Turn real-life situations into word problems that provide your child with math practice. For example, "If everyone eats two hamburgers, how many do I need?" or "If this shirt costs $7.99, how much change will I get back from $10.00?"

Estimate Give your child a tape measure or a ruler. Ask him or her to estimate the length of a common object, such as a key, a doorway, or an envelope. Then measure the object to find its actual length. Take the tape measure with you on trips to the beach, the park, or the zoo. Estimate measures of other objects even if you can't verify them. Your child will become better at estimation with practice.

Sharpen Skills School Zone's *Math 3* or *Math 4* workbooks can help sharpen math skills before a new school year. *Math Puzzles* is a fun way to keep math fresh in your child's mind.

Science Activities to Share

Summer and science go together. The outdoors is a fantastic classroom for reinforcing science skills such as observation, prediction, classification, analysis, and evaluation. Use some of Jim Arnosky's nature books as inspiration for outdoor activities. Examples include *Drawing from Nature* and *Crinkleroot's Guide to Walking in Wild Places*. Or check out *Sharing Nature with Children* by Joseph Cornell.

On rainy summer days, turn your kitchen into a science lab. For ideas, refer to *Bet You Can! Science Possibilities To Fool You* by Vicki Cobb and Kathy Darling. Or learn how everyday things work with David McCauley's funny and informative *How Things Work*.

Field Work Invest in a field guide that you and your child can use to identify things that grow, creep, fly, or crawl. The National Audubon Society has a line of books just for kids, called *First Field Guides*. The guides feature moisture–resistant covers. Titles include *Wildflowers, Rocks and Minerals, Birds, Insects, Weather,* and *Mammals*.

Natural Patterns Go on a hunt for patterns in nature. Look for designs in spider webs, flower petals, leaf veins, the arrangement of tree branches, wave patterns on the beach, and so on. Encourage your child to take photographs of particularly interesting patterns.

Science Scavenger Hunt Send the kids on a scavenger hunt. Make up a list of science-related items to find or identify. Suggestions include:

- leaf from deciduous tree
- empty shell
- evergreen needle
- pine cone
- moss
- weed
- rock with quartz in it
- feather

Make a Rain Gauge Make a rain gauge from an empty, clear plastic bottle. Use scissors to cut the top third from the bottle. Then invert the top and put it inside the bottom part of the bottle to make a funnel-like section. Use a ruler and a permanent marker to label the bottle with measurements in 1/4" increments, with 0 at the bottom of the bottle. Place the rain gauge in another container so it won't blow over. (A clay flowerpot works well.) Check the level of water each day, and then empty the rain gauge.

Indoor Fun School Zone's deluxe edition science workbooks are filled with fun activities and interesting facts. Titles include *Weather/Seeds & Plants; Insects & Spiders/Reptiles & Amphibians;* and *Mammals/Ocean Life*. These workbooks are great for rainy days, long car trips, or boring doctor's offices.

Social Studies Activities to Share

The social studies include geography, history, economics, citizenship, and government. The United States Department of Education has many ideas for building your child's social studies concepts. Visit their Web site (www.ed.gov/pubs/parents/learnact.html). The activities below will build children's understanding of social studies.

Go Back in Time Take a family trip back in time. Go to a restored village, a historical site, or a history museum. As you tour the location, talk about what was different long ago and what is the same today. Follow up by reading a story set in a historical village, such as *Sarah Morton's Day* or *Samuel Eaton's Day,* both by Kate Waters and both set in Plymouth Plantation. Or choose a family activity from *Colonial Days: Discover the Past with Fun Projects, Games, Activities, and Recipes* by David C. King.

Plot the Course Put your child in charge of the map for a family trip. Work together beforehand to go over the route. Then let your navigator be in charge of helping you follow the route accurately.

Traditional Thinking Every family has its own traditions. Talk about yours. Invent some Fourth of July traditions if you don't already have them. Let your child help in planning the holiday celebration by making special place cards, decorating napkins, and so on.

Have a Reunion Take advantage of summer weather to get together with your extended family. Before you go to the reunion, work with your child to create a family tree or a chart that shows the family relationships.

Live Like Long Ago No, you don't have to do without electricity. But you can have fun making a sweet treat just like people did long ago. Dry some fruit using sun power instead of the oven. Pitted cherries; seedless grapes; and sliced apples, pears, and peaches are all good choices. Spread plastic wrap over a cookie sheet. Then place the fruit on the plastic wrap in a single layer. Cover with cheesecloth and set in a sunny spot.

Recycle Put your child in charge of the family's recycling. Talk about what can and cannot be recycled in your community. Help your child set up a recycling center in the garage, basement, or kitchen. Then make a chart to keep track of how much is recycled over the course of the summer.

Plays Well With Others Your child will develop social skills and sharpen basic knowledge with School Zone's software and games. Check out www.schoolzone.com

Answers

Page 2

Al
homework
grasshoppers
basketball
fireworks
watermelon
afternoon

Kelsey
sunshine
sweatshirt
starfish
seashore
postcards
fireflies
daydream

Tori
rowboat
lifeguard
flashlight
weekend
sunflowers
thunderstorm

Matt
skateboard
baseball
campfire
downtown
skyscrapers
backyard
birthday

Page 3

1. seed
2. drain
3. pair
4. day
5. cot

6. pool
7. patch
8. lake

A triplet

Page 5

1. 12−3=8 NO
2. 12+1−5=8 YES
3. 8+1=12 NO
4. 6+1=8−1 YES
5. 2x1<6 YES

6. 1>1 NO
7. 8+1≠3+6 NO
8. 3x2=6=12 YES
9. 12÷2≠6 NO

Page 8

Answers will vary. Surveys should include seven responses.

Page 4

1 giraffe
3 elephants
8 wolves
2 lions
1 panda

6 camels
12 monkeys
5 snakes

Page 6

Page 7

1. Eddie
2. Koisha
3. Kelsey
4. Matt
5. Mike
6. Tori

Page 9

Page 11

1. watermelons (greatest), peas (least)
2. 22 feet
3. cauliflower by 2 feet
4. lettuce by 2 feet
5. 48 feet
6. 26 feet

Page 10

Plant Perimeters
Beans -18 feet
Cauliflower -14 feet
Potatoes -16 feet
Broccoli - 20 feet
Peas -10 feet
Watermelons - 22 feet
Pumpkins -16 feet
Carrots -14 feet
Spinach -12 feet
Lettuce -18 feet

Page 12

1. pages 13, 22
2. page 20
3. page 31
4. page 6
5. pages 5-6
6. page 25
7. pages 30-31
8. page 28
9. page 4
10. page 29

Page 13

	Good Guy	Bad Guy
earthworm	✓	
aphids		✓
cutworm		✓
earwig		✓
honeybee	✓	
hornworm		✓
Japanese beetle		✓
ladybug	✓	
slug		✓
spider	✓	
toad	✓	

Page 14

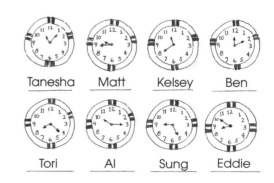

Tanesha Matt Kelsey Ben

Tori Al Sung Eddie

Page 15

1. flowers
2. sisters
3. birds
4. toys
5. boxes
6. benches
7. dresses
8. taxes
9. puppies
10. berries
11. cities
12. stories

pennies   parties
wishes   dresses
bears   eggs

Page 16

Answers will vary.

Page 18

U. 320   T. 438   H. 578
A. 86   Y. 161   P. 90
R. 402   0. 292   H. 40   F. 179   P. 135

Happy Fourth!

Page 21

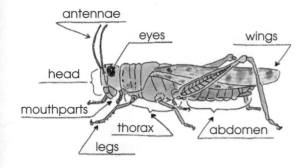

antennae, eyes, wings, head, mouthparts, thorax, legs, abdomen

Page 25

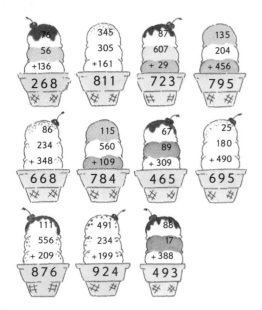

76	345	87	135
56	305	607	204
+136	+161	+ 29	+ 456
268	**811**	**723**	**795**

86	115	67	25
234	560	89	180
+ 348	+ 109	+ 309	+ 490
668	**784**	**465**	**695**

111	491	88
556	234	17
+ 209	+199	+ 388
876	**924**	**493**

Page 17

1. The (colorful) float moved <u>quickly</u>.
2. A (huge) crowd of people watched <u>happily</u>.
3. The (marching) band played a (merry) tune.
4. The (hot) sun made everyone move <u>slowly</u>.
5. A (striped) flag waved <u>wildly</u> from a (brick) building.
6. The (thirsty) kids bought (cold) drinks.
7. Everyone sat <u>comfortably</u> on the (soft) grass.
8. (Bright) fireworks soared <u>high</u> into the (inky) sky.
9. A (small) child cried when the fireworks exploded <u>loudly</u>.
10. A (cool) shower made the fireworks end <u>suddenly</u>.

Page 19

Eight examples should be marked.

Page 22

Note: Accept other answers if child can identify a logical pattern.

1. scallop
2. limpet
3. conch
4. mussel
5. snail
6. limpet
7. limpet
8. conch

Page 24

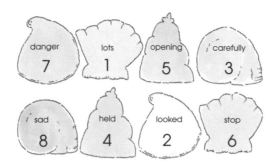

danger 7   lots 1   opening 5   carefully 3

sad 8   held 4   looked 2   stop 6

Page 20

Al's sandwich is the third from the left, layered as follows:

whole wheat bread
carrots
turkey
lettuce
whole wheat bread

Page 23

METAL 4   PAPER 3   PLASTIC 3

Page 26

Start in	Head	End up in
Illinois	east	Indiana
Pennsylvania	north	New York
Maine	southwest	New Hampshire
South Dakota	south	Nebraska
Nevada	west	California
Delaware	north	New Jersey
Oklahoma	south	Texas
Mississippi	northwest	Arkansas
Florida	northwest	Alabama
Colorado	west	Utah
Minnesota	east	Wisconsin
Connecticut	north	Massachusetts
West Virginia	northwest	Ohio
Oregon	east	Idaho

Page 30

1. Bus #45; 7:37 A.M. or 5:11 P.M.
2. 5 minutes
3. 59 minutes
4. 49 minutes
5. Bus #23 at 7:07 A.M. or Bus #45 at 7:37 A.M.

Page 32

1. great-grandfather
2. Anna O'Toole
3. Fred James
4. father
5. her grandmother, Victoria Reiser
6. two
7. Anna O'Toole
8. Joseph Rinaldi
9. Joshua Reiser
10. Eleanor Grady

Page 34

1. great
2. weather
3. fir
4. grown
5. beach
6. bare
7. meat
8. dessert
9. ate
10. chilly
11. allowed
12. hoarse

Page 38

Note: Children can use other words for the underlined words below.

1. Al underlined{asked}, "Which way is the lake?"
2. Kelly underlined{cried}, "I can't wait to go swimming!"
3. Kelsey underlined{yelled}, "Help! I stepped in poison ivy!"
4. Ed underlined{said}, "I can't find my tent."
5. Lisa underlined{asked}, "Do I have to carry this all week?"
6. Kay underlined{moaned}, "I'm homesick already."
7. Matt underlined{asked}, "Does anyone know where the Mess Hall is?"
8. John underlined{said}, "Let's roast marshmallows now."

Page 28

Tori spent $10.25 and had $1.75 in change.
Al spent $11.75 and had $0.25 in change.
Kelsey spent $9.25 and had $2.75 in change

Page 29

Answers may vary.

Sight	Hearing	Taste	Touch	Smell
4	5	2	1	3
6	7	10	8	
9				

Page 31

"Let's get on the bus right **now**," said Kelsey in a l**ou**d voice.

Al laughed. "Calm d**ow**n, Kelsey. It doesn't leave for another five minutes."

Tori spoke up. "If we wait, the bus will be too cr**ow**ded." Matt said, "Okay, okay.

Let's get on." They all sat d**ow**n and started to talk about their day.

"H**ow** did you like going up to the top of the bank building?" asked Kelsey.

"I felt like we were up in the cl**ou**ds when we got to the top!" said Matt.

"The best part of the day was the clam ch**ow**der we ate for lunch," said Al.

"I thought the best thing was the f**ou**ntain," commented Matt.

"There were more coins in there than I could c**ou**nt!" Al exclaimed.

Page 35

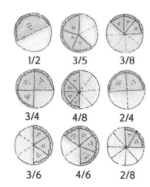

1/2 3/5 3/8

3/4 4/8 2/4

3/6 4/6 2/8

The four fractions are: 1/2, 2/4, 4/8, 3/6

Page 37

1. north
2. 2 miles
3. southeast
4. southwest
5. east
6. Catfish Lake
7. Mess Hall
8. 3 miles

Page 40

yes   no   yes
no   yes   yes
yes   no   yes
yes   yes   yes

Page 41

Answers will vary.
Notebook pages
should show sketches
and words.

Page 42

1. Tuesday
2. Saturday
3. Sunday
4. 10,413
5. 4,025

Page 45

1. 6 cups water, 2 cups lemon juice, 1 cup sugar
2. 4 quarts
3. 16 lemons
4. bottled lemon juice

Page 48

Answers will vary.

Page 49

1. cold
2. berries
3. hills
4. water
5. waves
6. rake
7. night
8. cats
9. noisemakers
10. school

Page 43

Note: Sentence completions will vary. The underlined phrases below are suggestions.

1. The fair/started on Monday afternoon.
2. Cows and horses/were in stalls in the barn. OK
3. The Ferris wheel/is 40 feet tall. OK
4. Kelsey's mother/won a blue ribbon. OK
5. The entrance booth/ was near the main gate.
6. An all-day ticket/cost four dollars.
7. Al/bought cotton candy. OK

Pages 46-47

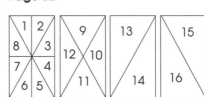

Page 44

Answers will vary.

Liquid
Lemonade
Water

Gas
Propane
Clouds
Smoke

Solid
Ice
Hamburgers

Pages 50-51

Page 52

16 triangles

10 squares

Page 53

Lane 1: 5 minutes
Lane 2: 2 minutes
Lane 3: 4 minutes
Lane 4: 3 minutes
Lane 5: 8 minutes
Lane 6: 10 minutes
Lane 7: 6 minutes
Lane 7: 3 minutes

Page 54

Answers will vary. Poems should follow the cinquain pattern.

Page 55

Answers will vary. Format and punctuation should follow the form of a friendly letter.

Page 56

Good Time Grocery
slippers
pretzels
bread
peanut butter
apples

Sports Store
basketball
backpack
apples
baseball
gym bag

Carl's Clothing Store
shorts
socks
T-shirt
pencils
blue jeans

Village Shoe Store
sandals
blue jeans
sneakers
boots
slippers

Office Supply Store
crayons
paper
gym bag
ruler
pencils

Grade 3 Summer Scholar **02234**